Jazz Practice Ideas
With Your Real Book

Jazz Practice Ideas
With Your Real Book

*Using Your Fake Book to Efficiently Practice Jazz Improvisation, while
Studying Jazz Harmony, Ear Training, and Jazz Composition*

For beginner and intermediate jazz musicians

ANDY McWAIN

FULLER STREET
MUSIC & MEDIA

The author greatly appreciates you taking the time to read his work. Please leave a review wherever you bought the book. Please visit: http://www.jazzpracticeideas.com to sign up for our mailing list!

Thank you for supporting my work.

First Edition: v.1.6
Published by Fuller Street Music & Media
Music Copyist: Brandon Carrita

For the love of my life and our little girl:
You two are so amazing. Thank you for everything.

Table of Contents

Jazz Practice Ideas 9

Introduction 11

CHAPTER ONE: About the Real Book 15

CHAPTER TWO: How to Use This Book 19

CHAPTER THREE: Big Picture: Developing Your Skills 21

CHAPTER FOUR: Your Daily Practice Routine 25

CHAPTER FIVE: Performance Practice and Sight Reading 29

CHAPTER SIX: Improvised Melodic Lines, Part I 33

CHAPTER SEVEN: Improvised Melodic Lines, Part II 45

CHAPTER EIGHT: Jazz Rhythm and Meter 53

CHAPTER NINE: Jazz Harmony 59

CHAPTER TEN: Ear Training 69

CHAPTER ELEVEN: Transcribing Solos 73

CHAPTER TWELVE: Foundations of Jazz Composition 77

CHAPTER THIRTEEN: Closing Thoughts 83

CHAPTER FOURTEEN: Jazz Listener's Guide 85

Bonus Charts 89

Your Opinion 93

Acknowledgments 95

Gratitude 97

About the Author 99

Author's Note 101

Jazz Practice Ideas

Thirty-Six Jazz Practice Ideas to Get the Most from Your Real Book

You may know about the REAL BOOK, but what you probably don't know is how much MUSICAL PROGRESS can be accomplished with only a single fake book!

Don't know what to practice? Don't want to waste valuable time? Based on years of university-level teaching, the author of this book gives jazz musicians:

- Simple, focused melodic, harmonic, and rhythmic strategies on how to use their limited practicing time more efficiently
- Easy-to-understand practice ideas for any jazz musician to apply over any real book tunes
- A blueprint of improvisation tips to avoid the pitfalls of directionless practicing

Here's the beginner/intermediate jazz strategy list you've never seen before:

Thirty-six actionable melodic ideas, harmonic ideas, rhythmic and metric tips, ear training exercises, and basic arranging and composition blueprints, and more...

- Do you know why many young musicians fail? Why intermediate-level musicians get stuck?
- Do you feel like the secrets of WHAT and HOW to practice jazz improvisation are out of your reach?
- Do you want to really deepen your connection to the music you play?

Sometimes jazz musicians want to get better, but don't always know how -- even with the help of a teacher. These thirty-six jazz practice ideas cover a wide range of modern jazz improvisation strategies, presented in clear topic chapters to provide the most effective results for beginner and intermediate players.

You want to know what to practice? Any real book or fake book tune.
Okay, now what? Choose one or more of these 36 actionable practice ideas (starting in Chapter 5) and make real progress with your musical abilities: improvisation and soloing, ear training, connecting harmony, and more.

For jazz piano, jazz guitar, jazz saxophone, jazz trumpet, jazz bass, jazz voice, jazz trombone, jazz drums, and all other improvising instruments.

Introduction

"He who would leap high must take a long run."
- Danish proverb

Jazz Practice Ideas with Your Real Book
Using your fake book to efficiently practice jazz improvisation,
while studying jazz harmony, ear training, and jazz composition
(for beginner and intermediate jazz musicians)

Leverage Your Real Book and Maximize Your Jazz Practicing Time

How many jazz real books and fake books do you own? Well, here's a beginner and intermediate jazz musician's practicing guide to get a lot more out of them! From improvisation strategies -- both melodic and harmonic -- to ear training and jazz composition, here is a collection of actionable steps, exercises, and ideas that you can use to get the most out of your jazz practice sessions -- all using your real book. [Intended for all instruments including jazz piano, jazz guitar, jazz bass, jazz saxophone, jazz trumpet, jazz trombone, jazz vibes, jazz drums, jazz vocalists, jazz arrangers and composers, and more.]

Aiming for more efficient jazz practice on a wide range of topics:

• Applied jazz harmony, and the structural ways to think about your material
• A range of modern jazz improvisation strategies: including tritonics, tetratonics, pentatonics, hexatonics, chromatic approach, blues scales, and more
• Practice strategies with rhythm, meter (including odd time signatures), and more

- Ear training and sight singing exercises -- all straight out of your fake books
- Jazz composition exercises: using the inspiration and the harmonic structure of jazz real book tunes (using contrafacts and other concepts)
- Planning your practice sessions (efficiency of time; practice in all 12-keys), and more...

Jazz musicians, especially beginner or intermediate players who are becoming serious about their playing, need a wide variety of ways to develop their improvisational abilities. The book is designed around thirty-six (36) practice ideas and jazz improvisation tips that connect a range of modern jazz study topics directly to your real book -- any real book, or jazz fake book.

◇ ◇ ◇

Welcome to my new applied jazz improvisation book! I've wanted to write this material for a long time -- and as a practicing musician, I think I always really wanted to read a book like this!

I put this material together so beginner and intermediate jazz musicians could have a more direct outlet to useful, actionable information in a shorter and less expensive format than many other jazz theory, improvisation, and harmony texts.

Why write this book now?

One reason is that real books are everywhere. Musicians, trying to build a library of the widest possible range of jazz tunes, already have quite an investment in their multiple volumes of real books. And I want to make sure that jazz musicians understand how any of these books can be more central to their daily practice.

The problem is that beginner and intermediate jazz musicians often see their various real books and jazz fake books as simply collections of tunes. To many students and young musicians I have encountered, these books are just a huge arsenal of songs and repertoire, and vehicles for improvisation on gigs, jam sessions, and/or recordings. Being prepared for any song, right? That is true! That's exactly what the real books are: massive collections of material perfect for jazz musicians to learn, play, internalize, and record. But they are also so much more.

There are some very creative ways to use any fake book to study all the main aspects of this music: creative improvisation, jazz theory, jazz harmony, ear training, basic arranging, and jazz composition. In these pages, we'll explore these strategies to be more comprehensive with your jazz practicing. We'll cover various practice topics, structured in 36 units which you can refer back to at any time, and in any order.

If you follow even some of these jazz practice ideas, you will likely not only get more benefit and enjoyment out of your fake books, but also seriously progress in your improvisational abilities.

But first, let's discuss the real book itself...

1

About the Real Book

"The artist who aims at perfection in everything achieves it in nothing."
- Eugene Delacroix

Obviously you can learn a jazz tune directly from the recording, or by playing along with others by ear; these are probably the best ways, leading to deeper connections to the material as players are forced to really listen from the start, without the distraction of reading music. That said, nearly every jazz musician owns at least one real book, fake book, or other music collection with basic chord symbols and melodies. Most musicians I know have several different copies and multiple editions of these fake books, even including the smartphone or tablet app, and ebook versions as well.

For music you don't know, haven't transcribed, or haven't learned by ear, fake books are essentially a shortcut to playing and practicing the music. The goal of course should be to learn and memorize the music as quickly as possible and not use these charts to perform. I know jazz musicians who already know hundreds of tunes who keep fake books only for reference. They might study a chart and recording at home, but unless they are playing original music, specific arrangements, or a really obscure tune, will never bring sheet music to a gig. Pianist Kenny Werner wrote in one of his books that he never plays a tune out on a gig that he hasn't really worked through, and or that he hasn't completely internalized.

This is our goal: use the fake books as we need, but aim to make the music our own as fast and permanently as we can.

There are many different versions of real books and jazz fake books, including the multiple volumes of the mainstream Hal Leonard Corp, Chuck Sher, and Warner Bros editions. There are also various artist-based books, such as those dedicated to the music of Miles Davis, John Coltrane, Bill Evans, Charles Mingus, Bud Powell, Charlie Parker, etc., as well as regional collections (Colorado, European, etc.), various transcription-based books, and a number of style-based fake books (Vocal, Dixieland, Latin, Christmas, and more). Many of these are available as play-alongs, in various apps, and are supplemented all the time with new versions based on key, clef, and more. Online, Amazon and eBay recently showed thousands of results for the search term "jazz real book"!

Most of these books are the legal, copyright-cleared versions made in the last several years. But the first time I bought a real book, I was in Boston and had been told to go to a small record store and ask for it at the counter, because these books were bootleg and not copyright-cleared and weren't even kept on the shelves. Publisher Hal Leonard Corp acknowledged the existence of these musician-only earlier volumes of the Real Book when they released their fully cleared and licensed first edition as the 'sixth' edition.

The jazz compositions in all of these books vary widely as well. From jazz standards considered part of the "Great American Songbook" tradition, broadway-based show tunes, various blues, and swing jazz classics, each real book hopes to give musicians enough music to play for several gigs! With newer additional volumes of fake books, the music of contemporary jazz composers reaching beyond the swing and bebop eras appeared widely for study and performance. These latest real books give players material to explore in post-bop, modal, (some) avant-garde, fusion, and a range of other more current modern jazz styles.

While the original real books had songs by George & Ira Gershwin, Cole Porter, Rodgers & Hart, Duke Ellington, Miles Davis, Thelonious Monk, Antonio Carlos Jobim, and Wayne Shorter, the newer fake books include more recent compositions by artists like saxophonist Kenny Garrett, pianist Brad Mehldau, guitarist John Scofield, saxophonist Michael Brecker, guitarist/singer Caetano Veloso, trombonist Conrad Herwig, composer/arranger Maria Schneider, saxophonist Sam Rivers, and others.

A couple generations ago it was likely possible for a jazz musician to learn all the tunes and standards necessary to play most gigs just by learning songs from recordings, and regularly performing with others. Now of course, with all the important branches, sub-styles, and sub-genres of jazz, we would never be able to get a roomful of jazz musicians to agree on which tunes a beginner improviser should know. (Many have tried!)

This is why most jazz gigs tend to gravitate to the same 100 to 200 standard tunes. And cities and regions even have a shared repertoire that many people tend to play. When I was in Shanghai a few years ago, everyone seemed to play the jazz standard Speak Low and the Wayne Shorter tune Yes and No, and some other common material across very different bands (instrumental and vocal). At the university where I teach, the jazz tunes Red Clay and Solar have often been in heavy rotation, being passed from player to player.

Young musicians should focus on expanding their repertoire, but need to just learn to play, to really improvise in the moment, and to be able to tell stories with their instruments without just learning the tunes. This development process is, of course, connected to the standard repertoire, but it's also about a deeper level of universal control over your instrument. It really seems like great players can improvise amazing solos over anything! (Check out all of Herbie Hancock's recent projects for examples of this!)

It's also interesting to note that many of the (younger) jazz recording artists are now focused on playing original tunes, music borrowed from other genres like rock, pop, metal, etc, in addition to songs from the mainstream jazz tradition. It seems that for many of these musicians, they're focused on demonstrating an individual sound and approach, not just their take on traditional repertoire. Today, it's possible for jazz musicians to know one hundred (100) jazz tunes and work as consistently as someone who knows (300) three hundred tunes! (Obviously, playing with jazz singers often requires more tunes, but those experiences really help build repertoire!)

So these Jazz Practice Ideas listed here apply to any beginner or intermediate jazz musician developing their improvisation abilities, control, and sound in any of the sub-styles of jazz, and can be applied to practicing inside any or all of these fake books or real books!

So you can have both! You can learn the standard tunes, and also develop a deep, personal journey toward fluent improvisations, internalized music, and spontaneous creation -- you can master and memorize the important jazz literature, while understanding the important components of applied jazz harmony, and composition.

So let's discuss how to use this book...

2

How to Use This Book

"He knows not how to know, who knows not how to un-know."
- Sir Richard Francis Burton

This book is a rather extensive list of practice ideas and tips -- over three dozen! -- to more efficiently use your real book(s), and to help you improve as a player and as a unique improviser. I want you to use this book to help you to gain more control, flexibility, and spontaneity with your instrument! And always remember "getting better is fun!" (Thanks, Charlie B.!)

So use this book in any way that helps you with your current jazz practicing, and that helps you make the most of your time. It doesn't really matter if you are currently taking lessons, enrolled in school, or completely self-taught, I have designed this book to try to help every jazz musician and new improviser with their current development.

So if you find at least one useful jazz practice idea, one improvisation tip, or one inspiring line in this entire book, then it's all worth it! And even though this should be a quick read once through, my hope is that you'll be able to refer back often for new practice ideas.

You can browse through these practice tips as they are organized here, or read them in any order you prefer, since I wasn't implying any sense of priority based on the numbering system. Each one is labelled and categorized in chapters based on melody, harmony, etc., but many of these topics continually overlap with other aspects of your musical skills, as well as practicing tactics, and strategies.

If you find something in this book that sounds familiar, that you've heard or read before, or that a teacher, fellow musician, or another player has told you, then simply nod to yourself with the knowledge that we all agree! Why is this important?

When I was first learning to play jazz, I appreciated the *confirmation* of hearing the same or similar advice from multiple sources to know that it was truly important. (And if you don't know, **Confirmation** is also a well-known bebop composition by alto saxophonist Charlie Parker. Don't worry, I won't sprinkle jazz titles throughout the text, that would get distracting!)

This book isn't intended to replace any other texts, methods, teachers, or programs. I consider this material a supplement to any and all of your other jazz resources, but wrote it because I wanted to open the discussion about better ways to use the real books that we all own!

Now let's discuss the big picture of developing your skills as a musician...

3

Big Picture: Developing Your Skills

"Never let the fear of striking out get in your way."
- George Herman ("Babe") Ruth

The main reason I've seen that new improvisers don't develop very quickly is that they don't really have a sense of how or what to practice. They generally try to learn tunes and attempt to solo over those tunes and many just repeat that process over and over again.

Beginner and intermediate jazz musicians and improvisers can actually get pretty serious and methodical about their development by simply structuring their practice time. So we need new ways to think about what you're working on.

How Do Aspiring Jazz Musicians Develop Their Skills?

Aspiring jazz musicians of any age often find it quite overwhelming to develop their improvisation abilities. They might have a clear sound in their mind, often from a favorite player or recording, and they cannot seem to recreate it on their instruments. They can't seem to reach a level of fluency where they can express themselves in the moment.

Because it takes years of study, practicing, playing and performances to achieve a certain level of mastery in any field, most accomplished players have developed focused ways of practicing to speed up the process.

Here is a way to "plan your work" and "work your plan" as a jazz musician:

The first idea is break down your practice time on your instrument into blocks. Plan to spend a certain amount of time just playing and improvising. If you only have an hour to practice in a single sitting, this open playing could just be ten minutes at the beginning of your practice session and another ten at the end. This leaves forty minutes of that first hour to really work on specifics. Real gains will be made when you devote some of your available practice time specific tasks like improvisation strategies or exercises, focused ear training, and transcribing and learning the solos by great players on your recordings.

If you have multiple hours throughout the day to practice, play, jam, and record, you should make a list of the skills and abilities that you wish to have and focus your effort s on studying the musical concepts that get you closer to your goals.

Jazz Theory and Jazz Harmony: It's always useful to spend some time exploring the fundamental theoretical basis for jazz including chords (tones & tensions), chord scales, modes and diatonic relationships [major, melodic and harmonic minor], harmonic analysis, forms (blues [12-bar and others], rhythm changes [based on Gershwin's "I Got Rhythm"], 32-bar AABA song forms, and through-composed tunes, etc.). These represent the color palette of your note, chord, and song choices as you play.

If you do this is in a personal way, you'll start to learn about the people involved in the history of this music, the cultural context, and the roots and threads of African American music that connect much of this together. You'll discover the spiritual and temporal aspects of music and see that jazz has long had an interesting balance of sacred and secular. You'll learn the lyrics of these pieces and have some idea of how to develop your music "as a storyteller," even if you're an instrumentalist exclusively.

Applying an improvisation strategy is essentially using jazz theory and harmony to help you in the creation of spontaneous solos. It's also a way to have some material to practice that helps you always have a launching pad for your solos. These strategies can be melodic, rhythmic, or harmonic and a number will be outlined here. You can learn ways to think about your solo improvisations through transcription studies, where you learn another musician's solos note-for-note (see Chapter 10 for a more complete discussion on transcribing).

Your short-term goals should include pattern-breaking, or changing things that you always seem to play that sound "stale" to you, and to develop a facility on your instrument in all 12-keys.

As an improviser, you also need to increase your musical reaction time, what I refer to as your "latency" period, which is defined as a time interval or delay between "stimulation and response." Think about it. You know what to do but you can't do it fast enough, or you take too much time thinking about your 'response' that you miss these moments entirely.

So I like to think that modern jazz musicians and improvisers regular blend three different approaches to their soloing. These blend the techniques of the earliest improvisers with the most modern concepts of total chromaticism (chroma= the Greek word color).

Here are the THREE PRINCIPAL APPROACHES of improvisation:

a) ear/fixed system - playing entirely by ear. This can be simply knowing or finding a key center and improvising only by adjustment, or playing from nothing and only listening for clues. The fixed system could also refer to something like a single blues scale played over all the chords of a blues, regardless of the changes in the progression.

b) chord scales - playing the underlying scale of the harmony. This is essentially a method, common in jazz education, where every chord symbol is translated into a scale or mode for the improviser. For example, A7 equals A-B-C#-D-E-F#-G, or A mixolydian, the fifth mode of D Major. Now I know enough to play up and down the basic scale for my chord symbol. Notice that this is essentially horizontal thinking.

c) chord tones (12-notes) - which is a modern approach to improvisation based on playing the underlying arpeggio (broken chord of R-3-5-7-9-11-13) as 'target' notes using any diatonic or chromatic approach notes. This is essentially a vertical approach and gives the player all twelve pitches of the chromatic scale to use at any moment.

As you make changes and progress in your playing, it's also useful to spend some time thinking about your practice techniques and any performance issues. This means focus on ways to improve the results from your practicing time, and increase your performance efficiency. All of these topics here work for a musician's self-study regimen, or for those working with a teacher and/or mentor. It also helps to keep a practice log to document your individual progress and your specific goals.

The top six fundamental goals for aspiring players in jazz improvisation should be the development of:

- consistently playing with a good sound and/or tone (instrument or voice)
- developing a solid time feel, groove, and 'deep' sense of swing
- possessing a deeper sense of hearing, listening, and ear training (as it relates to melodic, harmonic, and ensemble hearing)
- develop fluency on your instrument in all keys
- mastery of jazz tunes, repertoire, and material to be able to play with the widest possible range of improvisers
- writing material of your own -- compositions help to define a sound world for your improvisations -- and even if you have no compositional aspirations -- help you to recognize the art, mastery, and craftsmanship in other pieces

On top of all of that, we are trying to develop our ability to just play without thinking. We study these things to add them to our understanding of music, and to put them in our ears, but then we need to be able to let go and just improvise.

Next, let's talk about a simple way to deal with the issue of practicing in all 12 keys.

4

Your Daily Practice Routine

"If you start to take Vienna - take Vienna."
- Napoleon Bonaparte

If you don't know this already, fluency in all twelve keys is really the goal of every musician, and the sooner you start working on that fluency the better. A very simple way to ensure that you rotate equally through key centers in your practicing is to vary key centers by the day of the week. This way as you practice your daily warmups, scales, modes, arpeggios, key centers, vamps, voicings, and jazz tunes, etc., you will be more intentional about using a wider range of tonal centers.

If you already try to practice regularly in all keys, this practice grid might not be necessary for you, but it might still help solve a common problem. Even with the best plans to practice in all 12-keys, some players but don't finish that work in a single day. How many times have you started playing in the key of C, then G, then D, then A, then E, and before you can finish the circle of fifths, you need to stop practicing, and get on to some other part of your day? Even if your practice in each session moves up in half-steps (C, Db, D, Eb, E, F...), you still might not cover all 12 keys or give them equal attention.

With this chart below, any day you are practicing you simply refer to this chart and over the course of your week's practicing, you'll cover all 12-keys. (If you want to create your own plan just think six days in the week times times tonal centers, with a seventh day off or for makeup work). Put it up on your wall! And since you only have to focus on 2 key centers per day, you can actually spend more time in each tonality (major or minor).

◄ PRACTICE GRID ►

MONDAY	TUESDAY	WEDNESDAY
C, F#	D, Ab	E, Bb

THURSDAY	FRIDAY	SATURDAY
F,B	G, Db	A, Eb

◄ Sunday: day off/makeup ►

MONDAY: [Key of C] [Key of F#]
TUESDAY: [Key of D] [Key of Ab]
WEDNESDAY: [Key of E] [Key of Bb]
THURSDAY: [Key of F] [Key of B]
FRIDAY: [Key of G] [Key of Db]
SATURDAY: [Key of A] [Key of Eb]
SUNDAY: Day Off (and/or Key Makeups)

How does it work?

Okay, imagine it's Wednesday and I start to practice in the morning. Looking at the chart above I would see that I should focus my work on two different keys: E and Bb major/minor.

When I apply this practicing plan to my voicings, any scales, lines, exercises, arpeggios, and tunes -- it's plenty of work, but definitely more focused than trying to cover all 12 keys on that single day. It's also useful for those players mentioned above, with the best of intentions, whose 12-key work covers a handful of the same tonal centers each session before they must stop.

Throughout the course of natural practicing, you will randomly vary your work in all the major and minor tonal centers. With twelve keys -- at two keys per day -- that leaves a single day (Sunday, if you like) for makeups for any keys you have recently missed. But if you have a certain day that you never get to practice, it's possible that you can just adjust or rotate your key centers and make that your 'day off.'

Practice Routines

Whenever students ask about the best way to structure their practicing time, I always start by saying that there's no one answer that fits all musicians. You can start by figuring out what time of day or night that you seem to get the most work done, or seem most focused.

This is important because many young musicians assume that they are *night owls* or *'vampires'*, and only seem to find time to practice in the evening, or later into the night. This feels right in some ways because it makes a parallel between your practice session evenings, and any night gigs or concerts that you have. But it's just a cycle, pattern, or habit, and could be changed in a few weeks if you find a better way.

But if you actually track your practicing for a few weeks to a month, you might find that your longer, more focused practice sessions happen in the morning, or in the afternoon. (Write down the time you start to practice, what you worked on, and consider leaving some notes about how productive you think the session was.

You could even grade yourself on a scale like 1 to 5: one being 'frustrating' or 'unproductive', and five being 'very productive.' This info would only take a couple minutes at the beginning and the end of your practicing time, but will help you see patterns. Full practice logs make this whole process easier as well, and I recommend that everyone use a practice log or practice planner, whether they're self-teaching or in lessons.

For those who only practice late in the day, morning practice sessions are interesting psychologically because you begin your day with a sense of accomplishment. You already practiced -- before going to work, before school, and before your whole day. And for musicians trying to increase their daily and weekly practice hours, getting your first couple practice hours in the morning gives you a head start on your overall count for the day.

Try this:

Go into your practice session with a very specific agenda, and consider making some small advancement to your playing that's becomes permanent change to your abilities, sound, or overall understanding. This is different from the approach of practicing as "maintenance" or just chipping away at some insurmountable pile of musical work.

You could decide to learn a specific melody, play a line or voicing in all 12-keys, or something tangible like that, and not leave the practice room until that small goal is accomplished. (I always use the concept "now, play it all the way through, three times correctly," before I convince myself that I really have something down.

Here are a couple jazz practice routines that might be useful:

One hour sample practice routine: If you only have one hour to practice, keep your warm-up short, and then have a couple/few practice modules to work on, and then just allow yourself to play freely at the end. (This structure will help you keep from wasting the entire hour just jamming on some things you can already play, a very common problem.) These practice modules can be time just learning a tune, a technical exercise, or some specific work on an improvisation strategy (like the #1 - #36 here in this book).

Three hour sample practice routine: For players who find time [or should I say make the time!] for three, four, or five hours of practicing or more, one possible approach is to just scale up the single-hour template above with mini-breaks in between the hours. Another approach is to plan each additional hour with different modules and different goals, but still allowing yourself some time throughout for completely open and unstructured playing. Then as you continue playing, go back and review material that you practiced earlier to deepen your retention and control over it. But try to enjoy the work... As improvisers, we need to keep having fun while we practice, or the practicing really starts to feel grueling. I find that regular short breaks and some open improvising helps me refocus during the longer sessions. (If you consider yourself a 'connected' technology person, try blocking all email, text, phone calls, and messages until your break, or after you're done. Shut your phone or tablet off (ringer and vibrate), turn off wi-fi (block internet signal), or just try 'airplane mode' on some devices. Small portable electronic timers also help (don't use the one on your phone, if you can avoid it!). With a small timer, it's easy to stay focused if that's a problem you have while practicing.

Next up, let's get started with the thirty-six jazz practice ideas...

5

Performance Practice & Sight-Reading

*"If any man seeks for greatness, let him forget greatness
and ask for truth, and he will find both." -- Horace Mann*

Again, let me stress that since most students consider the jazz fake books simply a source for tunes and compositions to practice, for jam sessions, or on gigs, this book is about changing that. And of course, to be able to play these tunes on gigs and sessions, I know that players routinely practice these tunes right out of their real books. That's not our focus here.

What we are exploring together is the range of musical growth that can come from using these fake books and real books in other ways. For each of these thirty-six jazz practice ideas, I have created a separate description and title to give you an idea how you can apply it. But be creative!

You'll find that each is numbered to easily find them again. And for organizational purposes, they are divided up into chapters based on different aspects of our musical goals. Each of these is also marked with an indication whether it benefits all instruments, or is of particular importance to some instruments over others.

Here's how to apply these practice ideas: if I was working on a Herbie Hancock tune for an upcoming gig or concert, or just to learn for a jam session, I'd try to start by listening to a recording (or two) of the song (on iTunes, YouTube, Amazon, Spotify, or a physical CD/LP, whatever). I'd listen to the recording(s) a few times and try to catch parts of the melody on my instrument, while also listening/singing along with the bass player's roots and trying to hear the underlying harmony. The goal is to get as far as you can by ear. Be patient!

After a while, you look at the lead sheet to play and solo through the whole form (whatever you didn't learn by ear). Do this for several choruses. Afterwards you can choose an improvisation strategy -- or two-- from the list below to help you solidify the chord changes, reinforce the melodic content, and connect the harmonies together better for a more connected solo. I'm presenting it to you this way because many tunes I really listened to first, then learned, feel more grounded, while other tunes I read first, stayed at a distance for longer.

You'll also find that many of these 36 practice ideas stand on their own if you have no preset agenda for a portion of your practicing time. That can be pretty beneficial as well.

Jazz Practice Ideas
with Your Real Book:

#1
SIGHT READING EXERCISE BOOKS:

Start by realizing that the real book that you are carrying around with you is a great tool to practice SIGHT READING. Unless you have already played the 400+ tunes in most jazz fake books, then you'll find plenty of compositions to just open up and read down the chart.

For best long-term results, always sight-read with a slow but steady tempo, and do not stop for any mistakes that you make. Aim for a greater accuracy percentage with each new work that you read. Choose a solid tempo that you feel that you can play throughout the entire piece, scanning the entire chart for the fastest written subdivision before you begin.

Try not to look at sight reading as a pass-fail or all-or-nothing ability. If you can accurately play 58% of the notes you see on your first pass through a chart, strive for 60% on the next piece. The trick is pre-scanning the music for difficulty, key signature, and range, and then trying to never look at your hands while you read the music.

Bonus: Piano players have the possibility of by-passing the lead sheet chords, and just sight-reading the melody in both the right and the left hand together. FOR ALL INSTRUMENTS.

SUGGESTED TUNES: Try this with bebop heads by Charlie Parker, Dizzy Gillespie, Bud Powell, and Charles Mingus, as well as fusion tunes by Chick Corea, Michael Brecker, and others.

#2
INSTANT FULL ARRANGEMENTS:

Another level of sight-reading is the ability to create an entire arrangement on the spot. In addition to sight-reading (or sight-interpreting) the melody, a full arrangement would require additional comping, bass lines, or other aspects of texture to make the overall performance sound complete.

The focus here is to play a full arrangement of a tune, at sight, all the way through with the melody, a few choruses of improvised solo, and a complete out-chorus of melody. Focus on your time feel (swing or even-eighths), and the developing structure, direction, and contour of the overall form. This is the difference between practicing alone in a room, and the full-length 'telling a story' that happens in public performance.

It's really useful to do this type of practicing by imagining that you are on a gig and/or recording session and you can't stop, so whatever you play must be a completely realized version. FOR ALL INSTRUMENTS, BUT SPECIAL FOCUS FOR JAZZ PIANO/GUITAR

SUGGESTED TUNES: Start this with any tune that is potentially just beyond your reach. Why? The goal here is to stretch and expand beyond your current level and be able to create a solid version of any tune at sight. It's also useful to simply flip open a fake book to any page, and start to play a full set of music -- head/full solo/out head on each tune -- and then play the very next tune, and so on for an extended session (~ 45 minutes to an hour would be very productive). If you find a tune in your 'set' that you're too familiar with, skip it, and play tunes that are less familiar or more importantly, completely unfamiliar. Remember this is about making a complete statement every time -- even without any preparation -- and always landing on your feet.

Next up, let's look at several melodic-based improvisation strategies...

6

Improvised Melodic Lines, Part I

"Man falls seven times, stands up eight."
- Japanese proverb

As you have probably figured out already, connecting chord changes together is often the most difficult part of soloing. Combine this with the goal of a relaxed time feel, and facility all across your instrument, these are the biggest hurdles for new players. But one way to approach the practice of improvisation over chord changes is to use strategies that reduce the available notes in each jazz chord scales or harmony. That's some of what you'll find on this list.

For example, with a Cm7, after playing the entire 7-note chord scale (as dorian, aeolian, phrygian, etc), you can practice improvising on the sound of this chord by limiting your ideas to smaller groupings of the same scale: using only 6, 5, 4, 3, or 2 notes. This limitation allows you to really hear what you're doing and often go deeper with less notes than you might with the full scale or mode.

Here are the ways to improvise on a chord or sonority by playing these reductions (1-6 notes) of an entire 7-note chord scale.

- 1 note / single note: individual pitch (improvising by only playing single, disconnected pitches, leading to a kind of sparse, pointillistic playing.)

- 2 notes: intervallic playing (using a fixed system of intervals. For example, playing only the interval of minor sixth over all the harmony for a segment of your solo.)

- 3 notes: tritonic playing (3-note shells primarily based around scale degrees R25 and R45 including all diatonic possibilities. The frame of the perfect fifth adds to their flexibility in any situation. (This is not to be confused with the harmonic basis of many of John Coltrane's compositions which have three tonal centers or three tonics). (See Practice Idea #4 below)

- 4 notes: tetratonic shapes with three chord tones and one tension (M/Dom 1235; m/half dim 1345). (See Practice Idea #5 below)

- 5 notes: pentatonic (all reduced to their minor versions; for example F major = Dm pent). In minor, the pentatonic scale contains four chord-tones and one tension. (See Practice Idea #6 below)

- 6 notes: hexatonic or double triad (and all the diatonic expansions). Playing six notes of the underlying harmony, but as a simple pairing of two basic triads. (See Practice Idea #7 below)

- 7/8 notes: the complete chord scale (seven pitches in most modes or scales, and eight notes in the octatonic, symmetrical diminished scales). This is essentially a linear approach (root to seven), but is also vertical when you focus on the embedded diatonic seventh chords. (See Practice Idea #3 below)

-

#3
EMBEDDED DIATONIC SEVENTH CHORDS:

Most jazz musicians understand the power of practicing basic chord scales. Jazz theory and harmony was taught this way for a long time. Each chord on a chart has a specific chord scale that activates the complete, available sound of the harmony.

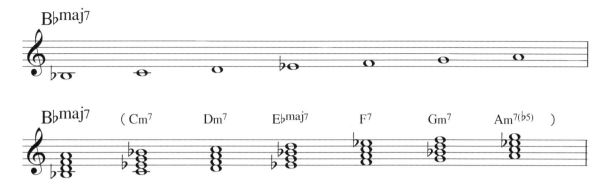

If you see a BbMaj7 chord, thinking chord scales you would practice a Bb major scale: Bb-C-D-Eb-F-G-A-Bb, or Bb Ionian mode. But a powerful extension of practicing chord scales is playing the embedded diatonic seventh chords inside this Bb major scale.

That requires stacking a full seventh chord on each scale degree. So over a vamp on BbMaj7 (also written BbM7) you can use melodic lines based on the arpeggios and connections of BbM7, Cm7, Dm7, EbM7, F7, Gm7, and Am7b5, all constructions made from the major scale, but each focused on a different sound. Think about it: we have two major seventh chords, three minor seventh chords, a dominant seventh chord, and a half-diminished or minor seventh flat-five chord! All of that is inside our major scale, but restructured vertically. FOR ALL INSTRUMENTS

SUGGESTED TUNES: Start by playing this on modal jazz tunes like So What, Impressions, Little Sunflower, and also on tunes that have single chords that last for at least four or eight bars like Recordame, Invitation, Saga for Harrison Crabfeathers, and others. After that it can be applied to any tunes you're working on, even those with a faster harmonic rhythm.

#4
TRITONICS:

Another way to pull out interesting things from the underlying harmony is to only focus on three-note groupings called tritonics. Think of these generally like a perfect-fifth frame (P5) with an additional note next to the root or next to the fifth. So we get R-2-5 ('R' means root!), and R-4-5 as the basic 3-note shapes. These are powerful as you move them diatonically through a key center.

For example, in Cmaj7, the useable (diatonic) tritonic groupings on R25 would be built on C (C-D-G), D (D-E-A), G (G-A-D), and A (A-B-E). Notice we usually skip the R25 shape in Cmaj7 that starts on scale degrees three, four, and seven: E, F, or B. This would give us E-F-B or F-G-C, or B-C-F which gives the 11 on a major chord, a "handle with care" note, and a half-step relationship between R and 2 on a couple of them. (These notes could be altered to #11 naturally, but that wouldn't maintain the diatonic structure of C ionian.)

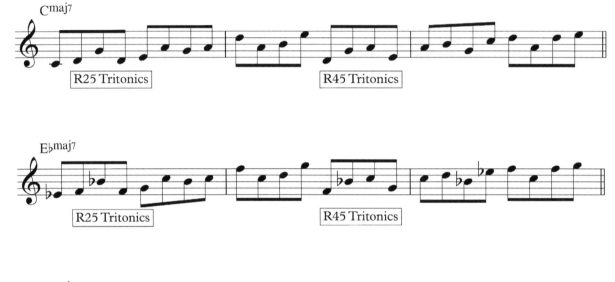

For the R-4-5 pattern, Cmaj7 gives us material on D (D-G-A), E (E-A-B), G (G-C-D), and A (A-D-E). Notice that these give us little melodic fragments of 9-5-13, 3-13-7, 5-R-9, and 13-9-3. We left out those R-4-5 shapes built on the root C, F, and B, which brings up the natural eleventh issue and half-steps again.

Of course, since all of the notes generating these tritonics are in the key, actually there is a case to sometimes use any or all of these shapes! Be sure to run these through all chord qualities. FOR ALL INSTRUMENTS

SUGGESTED TUNES: At first, try this on tunes with not too many chord changes like Blue Bossa, Alone Together, Take the A Train, Song for My Father, and Meditation, for example.

#5
TETRATONICS:

In his improvisations, saxophonist John Coltrane (1926-1967) regularly used a four-note pattern (or shape) over chord changes which makes a great practice exercise to take through many tunes in your real book. This four-note pattern is called a tetratonic, or also sometimes referred to as a melodic structures (by saxophonist Jerry Bergonzi, and others).

How to apply it: choose any major chord or dominant seventh chord and play the root, the second (or ninth), the third, and the fifth (R235). For minor chords, play the root, minor third, fourth (or eleventh), and the fifth (R345). In both cases, by playing these on chord changes you are automatically playing three chord tones and a tension (the 9 in major/dominant and the 11 in minor/min7b5).

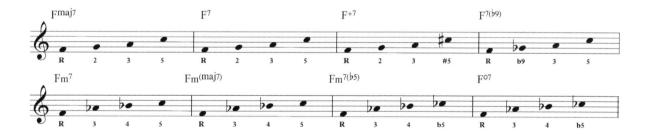

This is powerful because applying this tetratonic formula R235 or R345, you have something that works(!) to play on every chord change and on every beat. This is also good for technique, building tempo control, and for practicing your swing time feel.

The best way to play these through a fake book is to play continuous (1/8) notes and just repeat (or permutate) the chord if there is only one chord per bar. For the progression FMaj F6 | Em7b5 A7, the tetratonic line would be (all eighths): F-G-A-C and F-G-A-C in the first measure, and E-G-A-Bb and A-Bb-C#-E in the second.

Played through an entire song, it becomes a great exercise for reinforcing jazz harmony, swing time feel, continuous momentum, and more. After the basic shape becomes too easy, change the order of any of the numbers (permutation), and then take that pattern through a number of charts. For example R235 and R345, would be played 532R and 543R backwards. FOR ALL INSTRUMENTS

SUGGESTED TUNES: Start with standards that have busy chord changes like I'm Old Fashioned, It Might As Well Be Spring, and Have You Met Miss Jones, then move on to bebop tunes like Blues for Alice, Line for Lyons, and others. After that try tunes like Coltrane's Countdown, 26-2, Giant Steps, Chick Corea's Humpty Dumpty, or Kenny Barron's Voyage, among others.

#6
PENTATONICS:

It is also very productive to simply focus your playing on a fake book tune entirely on one improvisation strategy like the pentatonic scale, a 5-note grouping that is just another smaller collection of the available notes of the chord scale. Like some other jazz resources, I prefer to convert all pentatonic relationships to minor. Take your jazz charts, and apply the pentatonics throughout the entire forms for your improvisation practice.

For minor pentatonics, the basic pattern is R-m3-4-5-m7. Notice that it is a full (R357) arpeggio, plus the eleventh, or four chord-tones and a tension. For minor chords, apply the pentatonic as written, and also try the cycle of P5 pentatonics above. For example, on a Gm7, use Gm pentatonic (G-Bb-C-D-F), but then later try Dm pentatonic (D-F-G-A-C, or 5-7-R-9-11 over Gm7), up a P5 to an Am pentatonic (A-C-D-E-G, giving us 9-11-5-13-R over Gm7), and so on.

38

For ii7-V7 progressions, the same pentatonic can work for both chords. Over Gm7 to C7, the Gm pentatonic is obviously R-3-4-5-7 over Gm, but gives us 5-7-R-9-11 over the dominant chord. Up a perfect fifth, would yield Dm pentatonic over Gm7 to C7, and give us D-F-G-A-C or 9-11-5-13-R over the C7.

To apply the pentatonic to major chords, use the relative minor as your starting point. For example, CM7 followed by Am7 would both be 'converted' to an Am pentatonic. After improvising for a while on a relative-minor pentatonic, players should move pentatonics up by a P5 to try other collections.

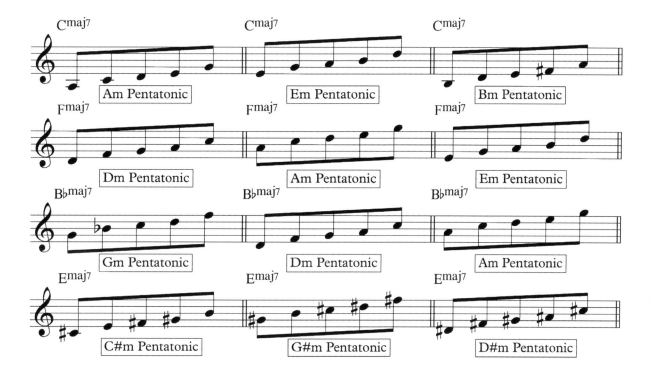

The next relationship would be CM7 to Am, using an Em pentatonic, then a Bm pentatonic, F#m pentatonic, C#m pentatonic, and so on. (In the first example, over CM7, Am pentatonic creates a collection of 6-R-9-3-5, with Em pentatonic over CM7 the chord tones 3-5-6-7-9 are available. With Bm pentatonic over CM7, we get 7-9-3-#11-13. Explore these relationships with all chord types: major, minor, dominant, etc.

Bonus: Notice that the basic minor pentatonic with an added #11 becomes the blues scale (see Practice Idea #11). This makes it easy to pivot back and forth between the two approaches. For a more advanced approach, I will also practice adjusting notes of the pentatonic by a half-step to fit other chords (altered dominant chords, for example). If you take an Am pentatonic (A-C-D-E-G), and you move the pitch D down to a C# to get A-C-C#-E-G, that becomes 13-R-b9-3-5 over a C7 chord, or R-#9-3-5-7 over an A7. FOR ALL INSTRUMENTS

SUGGESTED TUNES: Try this on tunes like Summertime, Triste, Old Devil Moon, Little Sunflower, Chega De Saudade, Cold Duck Time, Eiderdown, and 500 Miles High, among others. What you're looking for is tunes with a few single chord change that last long enough to be melodic with the pentatonic, or slower harmonic rhythm.

#7
HEXATONICS:

Hexatonics, also referred to as double triads, are a great way to expand your sound world over chord changes. If your playing on real book tunes often sounds like you're only mainly step-wise, scalar passages (all seven notes running up or down), then a six-note hexatonic collection will give you more intervals and leaps in your lines.

You can choose the two triads based on any two diatonic chords next to, or adjacent to each other in your scale. For example: F7 is a dominant scale, mixolydian, that is played F-G-A-Bb-C-D-Eb-F. When you stack triads on each scale degree you get F, Gm, Adim, Bb, Cm, Dm, and Eb.

To get a hexatonic sound you would play on F7, but use any side-by-side pair of triads from our list like Cm and Dm, or F and Eb, or Gm and Adim. The chords Cm and Dm (over F7), give you 5-b7-9 and 13-R-3, and that's how you should you hear these. F and Eb triads give you the R-3-5 and 7-9-11, and the Gm and Adim triads give you the 9-11-13 and 3-5-7.

(The example above also shows the same hexatonic pairs over A7, Db7, and G7 as well.

Once you practice these as ascending and descending triads, then go ahead and mix them up, trying different permutations and combinations -- and even writing out some useable lines. (See Practice Idea #33)

This concept, with all the possible hexatonic double triads, also works great as a basis for comping on piano, guitar, or vibes. For example on a G7 chord, a pianist could play a spread of the Dm and Em triads above as a voicing. This six-note chord is essentially the entire chord scale minus a single pitch, and with theses two triads, it gives us the 5-7-9 and the 13-R-3 of the G7. This is an example of applying one of my favorite phrases: all lines are chords, and all chords are lines. FOR ALL INSTRUMENTS

#8
CONTINUOUS ARPEGGIOS:

To build up both a solid sense of jazz harmony, and the ability to play long lines over changes in either swing or even-eighths time feel, players should regularly play through tunes in their real book with full 4-note arpeggios on each chord. (Go ahead and play the arpeggio twice if there is only one chord in the measure.)

This means that a single measure containing Bbm7 to Eb7, for example, would be played Bb-Db-F-Ab to Eb-G-Bb-Db in all eighth notes. For Am7b5 to D7b9, the line would be A-C-Eb-G to D-F#-A-C in eighth notes. With chords in root position, the lines can still be quite interesting because of the natural overlap. For example, in the Bbm7 to Eb7, the first arpeggio ends on Ab and then it's easiest to drop down a P4 to start the next chord. That connecting interval is what will make these sound less like an exercise, even though that's what it is. Remember that you're always embedding the sound of the changes of a specific real book tune into your ears, and sharpening your ability to quickly sound any chord.

If this exercise is too easy, it also makes a great speed metronome drill with fake book tunes that have two or four chords in every bar. Try increasing your tempo -- with a metronome if you'd like -- but always focusing on keeping your time solid, and your tone smooth. FOR ALL INSTRUMENTS

#9
ARPEGGIO PERMUTATIONS:

For the next level of difficulty with arpeggios, try playing them in various permutations. This means reordering the pitches inside the arpeggio. So instead of R357, try 753R, 357R, 573R, 3R57, and more. (Two dozen in all!) This is a great reinforcement of jazz harmony because you are not always building a chord up from the root, but instead can immediately move to the inner notes.

For an example of 3R57 on a measure containing Em7b5 and A7b9, using all eighth-notes, the line would be G-E-Bb-D to C#-A-E-G, which is quite musical and not like an exercise at all.

Once I begin an exercise like this, I like to just flip through a number of tunes in my real book (or in my head), and just keep playing the same permutations for a while. For every instrument, this exercise presents its own technical challenges, which is why it's useful. This is also a great exercise to practice with another player because it forces you to think ahead and helps catch any errors when your pitches don't match. FOR ALL INSTRUMENTS

7

Improvised Melodic Lines, Part II

"The way of success is the way of continuous pursuit of knowledge."
- Napoleon Hill

#10
CHROMATIC APPROACH:

Listening to great improvisers, one of the first things that you hear in their solos is the command of chromaticism. This is because they have direction to their lines with target notes in mind, and then there are countless ways to approach any pitch. Once you have played each available diatonic note that leads to your target, then you want to make a pass where you arrive at each note (the R-3-5-7-9-11-13) by passing through some chromatic approach tones. There are so many that I'll just give you a few to get started.

Try approaching each note by a half-step above or below and then to your target note; a half-step below, then a half-step above and then to your target; a half-step above, then a half-step below and then your target; two half-steps above or below, or a half below, two above and then to your target (or the opposite: half-step above, two half-steps below to the target note. You get the idea. And of course there are so many more possibilities!

Here is a G7 chord written out as R-3-5-7-9-11-13 for the target notes, indicated here by the whole notes. The other notes demonstrate four different approach patterns to the chord tones and tensions of G7 or G13, if you prefer.

Those give you some different examples of chromaticism, but there really are so many other approach patterns. They decorate the target pitch and delay its arrival, which often helps move chord tones to strong beats in the measure.

When you first play these lines, they may sound wrong. That's where you have to really focus on the intended target note and almost create a hierarchy in the way you present approach and destination pitches.

Try also discovering some chromatic approach patterns found in your favorite players' recordings. This is one of the benefits of transcribing. (See Chapter 10.) Chromatic approach ideas and different sounds are also possible to discover in the many published jazz solo transcription books available. FOR ALL INSTRUMENTS

#11
MINOR BLUES SCALES:

A very effective approach for jazz improvisation has always been to draw on the deep well of music that is the blues. You can emulate some blues-tinged sounds by playing a blues scale (in minor: R-b3-4-#4-5-b7) and the note-bends, inflections, and crunchy sound that goes with that. Although beginner's could simply apply the blues scale over a blues form (12-bar, 16-bar, or 24-bar are most common), it's also very productive (as a practice technique) to attempt to create a blues inflection over any tune.

The blues scale, in its similarity to the minor pentatonic, has proven to be a very effective collection of notes for very melodic playing. For many players, this is the main lesson that comes from practicing the blues scale.

Like the pentatonic, think of the blues as always minor and experience the sounds of applying it in different ways. For example: over a G7 twelve-bar traditional blues, it's possible to play Gm blues scale through all the changes (G7, C7, and D7), as well as changing to C and D blues scales for those IV7 and V7 chords.

It is also possible to play the blues scale up a perfect fifth (P5), and play a Dm blues scale on the entire G7-C7-D7 blues form. By extension, it's also possible to play each tonic blues scale up a P5 as well (so Dm blues over G7; Gm blues over C7, and Am blues over D7). Experiment here with the different sounds and colors.

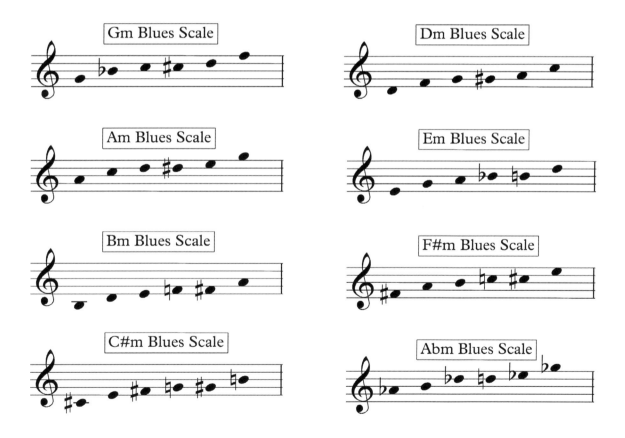

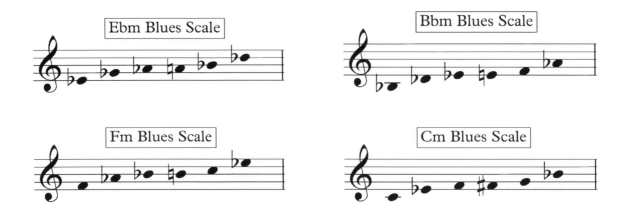

Thinking blues scales as minor, a GMaj7 chord could be given an Em blues scale (E-G-A-Bb-B-D). From there, I also cycle up by perfect fifths (P5) to get more possibilities. Over GMaj7, after Em blues (giving the 13-R-9-#9-3-5 of G major), I would also practice Bm blues scale (B-D-E-F-F#-A, giving us 3-5-13-7-maj7-9 over our G) and F#m blues scale (F#, A, B, C, C#, E, which gives us Maj7-9-3-11-#11-13 over G), C#m blues scale, Abm blues scale, Eb minor blues scale, and so on.

As you keep moving further away from the key center, the blues sound is still intact, but the new superimposed scales add more fresh pitches. Be sure to experience these sounds on a wide variety of chord types. And don't hesitate to seek out a number of authentic blues recordings to get a better sense of the feel, the players, and the cultural and social context. If you start at the beginning, recordings of Huddie Ledbetter, Robert Johnson and Bessie Smith will help. FOR ALL INSTRUMENTS

#12
COMMON TONE IMPROVISING:

A great exercise for expanding your ability to apply your knowledge of jazz harmony is common tone soloing. This is powerful because it helps beginning improvisers connect different chords and harmonies together, and also build up your skills at playing over the bar line. (This is similar to an exercise where you play one note over several chords, until you have to change!)

For example, with the chord progression Am7b5 to Ab7 to Gm7 to C7b9, we want to find common pitches that work throughout the progression, and on all four chords. While this approach is about your fluency with jazz harmony and ear training, the application here is for melodic lines.

Facility with common tone soloing is very helpful to launch a solo, for sustained notes, for bass pedal notes, and even helps with jazz composition. For the progression above, the pitch "C" works on all four chords -- it's the third of Am7b5; the third of Ab7, the eleventh of Gm7, and the root of C7b9. The pitch "Bb" works as well. On the first chord, using the locrian mode, Bb is the nine on Am7b5, and its the nine on Ab7, the third on Gm7, and seventh on the C7b9.

For jazz bass players, the ability to do this quickly and in the moment can help generate very exciting and modern sounding pedal tones. Even with chord changes moving above in a comping instrument (like guitar, piano, or vibes), that single common pitch pedal tone in the bass implies a sense of suspended time that really contrasts walking bass. FOR ALL INSTRUMENTS, BUT SPECIAL FOCUS FOR JAZZ BASS

#13
NEWLY AVAILABLE & COMMON TONES:

The opposite of the common tone approach becomes apparent with this kind of practice: finding the notes that are newly available as the chords change.

For example, as a Gm7 moves to the C7b9 there are many notes in common, but as we look at what new, fresh notes, colors, and sounds are available in the second chord, we recognize that the the pitches Db, Eb, and F# becomes available, for example (using the symmetrical diminished chord scale).

So an interesting approach is to mix the two (#12 and #13) where the common tone between Gm7 and C7b9 could include using the pitch "G" which works on both chords, and the shifting pitches of D on the first chord moving to a Db on the second. FOR ALL INSTRUMENTS

#14
LIMITED RANGE SOLOING:

One way to expand your ability to create chromatic, connected, and compelling improvised lines over a jazz tune is to limit your solo to a very small fixed range. It doesn't actually matter where this range falls on your instrument, just that it's kept to a small area like a perfect fifth (P5) or a perfect octave (P8), which are the two simplest ranges to remember.

Essentially however, this "limited range playing" can be any interval: a major sixth (M6), major seventh (M7), major ninth (M9), or an eleventh, for example. What does this do? This requires the improviser to connect harmony together by folding lines over to stay within the fixed area, using more repeated notes, and often more chromatic approach material. It's very instructive to see all the available choices within a very narrow and compact area of your instrument. FOR ALL INSTRUMENTS

#15
SIDE-SLIPPING CHROMATIC BI-TONALITY:

Another step to incorporating more chromaticism into your playing is to integrate bi-tonality into your lines. This is accomplished by the relationship of the original harmony, supported in the entire band or with comping alone, to lines and melodies in a new key. Originally referred to as "side-slipping," improvisers moved up or down from the original key for parts of their improvised lines.

But considered as polytonality, moving riffs, scales, and full melodic lines up or down by a major or minor second, or up or down by a major or minor third creates a lot of interesting sounds, colors, and textures in your solos. Listen for this in a number of great jazz recordings and transcribe for the different ways it can be done.

Bonus: Some modern players even pivot their lines around the diminished cycle, meaning at pitch, up a tritone, and up and down a minor third or the whole-tone cycle meaning up or down a major third. Try it out to hear what this sounds like. FOR ALL INSTRUMENTS

#16
IMPROVISING MELODIC SHAPES:

One way to play through real book tunes without spending so much time thinking about scales and chords, or improvisation strategies is to just approach your soloing with shapes. Imagine melodic figures that rise up and then fall back. Imagine playing zig-zags, where the intervals change direction.

This exercise has no limits because these can be literal geometric shapes like squares, rectangles, circles, rectangles, and more - or more abstract shapes, lines, curves, and more.

Once these shapes have been internalized, the development of the lines can include permutations of the notes that make up the shape -- essentially keeping the shape intact but starting in a different place. This whole helps players begin to visualize the contour of their motives, lines, and entire improvisations, leading to greater control in the moment. FOR ALL INSTRUMENTS

8

Jazz Rhythm and Meter

"Let him that would move the world first move himself."
- Socrates

As much as a lot of the material in this book is melodic, I've come to believe that rhythm is the most important aspect of improvising. If your ideas have strong rhythmic content, and a strong groove or sense of swing, the notes matter less and less. I can't stress enough the value that listening has for this part of your development. It's the language we're learning, and you must hear it played fluently.

#17
CHANGING TIME SIGNATURES AT SIGHT:

Here's a metrical exercise that's actually very liberating. It has the effect, for me, of making many tunes sound fresh again, and opens up many possibilities for new arrangements.

Essentially, a more advanced level of "sight reading" in jazz is the ability to read a chart in its current time signature, but perform the tune in another meter. A good example of this for the beginning jazz musician is the ability to play a song composed in 4/4, in the time signature of 3/4. If you want, it's pretty good to start this exercise with ballads.

Generally for 3/4 over 4/4, the two obvious approaches are that every full bar of four beats becomes three, or that each half of 4/4 becomes a bar of 3/4 time.

For more experienced, intermediate players, the possibilities here are endless, including the very useful modern jazz skill of being able to perform any tune -- at sight -- in 3/4, 4/4, 5/4, 6/8, 7/4, etc.

Generally this is accomplished by first lining up the original beat one (as written) with the new beat one in your new meter, and stretching or contracting the rest of the music into the rest of the time you have. If you do this, and always line up with beat one, interpretation of the melody becomes much easier as well.

The great benefit here is about expansion of your metric palette and building up new material and vocabulary in other time signatures. Once a musician struggles, battles, and conquers these conversions, without actually re-notating any of the charts, the return to playing only in 4/4 (or 3/4) becomes much easier and much more grounded. That alone is worth the effort. FOR ALL INSTRUMENTS

SUGGESTED TUNES: Try this on tunes you either no very well, or pretty much not at all. Both approaches are beneficial. Try My Funny Valentine, Lullaby of Birdland, I Didn't Know What Time It Was, Just in Time, or tunes that you feel are dated and maybe could use a refresh, like Let's Fall in Love, Stardust, S'Wonderful, or Three Little Words, for example.

#18
SAME RHYTHMIC IDEA THROUGHOUT

Another way to move your focus away from focusing too much on pitches or harmony is to decide on a basic rhythmic riff, and play it though an entire solo. As you improvise, your rhythmic idea is now fixed so you'll just choose notes as the chords change.

Although it's possible to also play a few scalar passages to connect material together, the benefit of this comes from trying to find ways to play your rhythmic idea everywhere in the song, even if you displace it in the measure.

Where can you find these rhythmic ideas? You can invent them spontaneously beforehand or make them up as you play. You can also borrow a motivic melody from the current jazz composition your playing in your fake book, or you can grab the rhythmic phrase from a recording of your favorite improviser. It doesn't even have to be from the same tune, it just has to be a strong, distinctive rhythm.

This last part is essentially rhythmic transcription, but you're not concerned with the actual pitches of the riff, although you can notate the rhythmic ideas that really speak to you. FOR ALL INSTRUMENTS

#19
CONTINUOUS IMPROVISED SUBDIVISIONS:

One practice strategy that helps players develop increased abilities playing over changes is to choose a jazz chart and then, after playing through the melody, to play a continuous line improvised solo. This is also a very effective way of working on your tone or touch (all instruments) and your overall time-feel (swing or even-eights).

Start with half-notes in 4/4 time, playing two improvised notes per bar. (In 3/4, play a dotted-quarter.) You can improvise several choruses this way, reinforcing all the available note-choices in the harmony, as well as voice-leading through the changes of your improvised lines, with solid placement in the measure (in 4/4 two half-notes on beats one and three). It's possible later to displace these half notes so that they start on beats two and four of a 4/4 measure.

Then play several choruses of soloing using all quarter-notes (in 4/4 or 3/4), which aligns the soloing with walking bass and the attack of beats 2 and 4 on the hi-hat in an ensemble. This can really help a new jazz player's time feel.

From there, continuous eighth-note (1/8) and sixteenth-note (1/16) force the player to make more note choices in each measure. Try these at comfortable tempos at first, maintaining both the complete line, and the correct melodic choices for the underlying harmony.

Continuous playing should also include practice sessions with the triplet versions of these as well. Triplet half-notes requires 3:2 playing, or three half-note choices in the space of two. In 4/4 time, this would mean three half-notes in each bar and the same relationships with triplet quarter-notes (for ex., two groups of three quarter-notes in 4/4 time), eighth-note triplets, sixteenth-note triplets, and so on.

Editing makes the exercise very fun, and more realistic to actual performance demands. Once you can play these lines continuously, in perpetual motion, then simply leave some notes out and begin to edit. For many players this is accomplished just by lifting their hands off of their instruments, or taking the mouthpiece away out of their mouth! Experiment with different notes being omitted rather than the same pattern, and emphasize playing over the bar line, and only stopping briefly once a new chord change has been reached. FOR ALL INSTRUMENTS

#20
SHIFTING CONTINUOUS SUBDIVISIONS:

Taking #19 as a starting point, improvisers should then practice playing continuous subdivisions, but shifting freely between them without breaking the line. For example, starting a continuous improvised line in all 1/8 notes, try seamlessly switching to quarter-notes, and then back again. Then perhaps switch to eighth-note triplets, back to eighth-notes, and so one. Many players find subdividing to a "faster" or small unit easier, but you also need to be able to smoothly and accurately move to a larger, or "slower," subdivision.

Once you can do this shifting continuous subdivisions continuous, then you should eventually add in the element of editing your lines. The goal is to try to leave notes out within a specific subdivision, but still connect to the next without any breaks.

If you edit your lines too close to the edges, and then shift, you'll lose the shifting effect. This exercise is great for your technique, and often sounds like a freely improvised solo without any practice strategy at work. FOR ALL INSTRUMENTS

9

Jazz Harmony

"Never let the fear of striking out get in your way."
- George Herman ("Babe") Ruth

#21
YOUR REAL BOOK AS A TRANSPOSING WORKBOOK:

A challenging use of a jazz fake book is as a transposing workbook. If you play a transposing instrument like saxophone (Bb/Eb) or trumpet (Bb), you already know what your principal interval of transposition should be. But every jazz musician should begin the process very early of attempting to play in all twelve keys. To practice this with your real book, you can play a jazz composition in its original key and then play the melody again in another key.

Musicians generally start with a M2 (up/down), m2 (up/down), m3 (up/down), or M3 (up/down). Feel free to experiment and choose any intervals. Although it seems largely like an intellectual exercise, this is generally a powerful combination of jazz harmony knowledge and concentration combined with ear training.

Finding other keys for Real Book tunes is really amazing for your ears, especially if you just recreate the pieces intervallically, but it can also be a useful sight-reading skill. Feel free to work on this skill away from you instrument as well, by just moving the changes, or notes, in your creative imagination. FOR ALL INSTRUMENTS

#22
TRANSPOSE THROUGH CHORUSES:

An extension of the transposition strategy is to play the melody of each piece in the original key and then take each chorus of improvisation in a different key. For example a piece written in C would be played in C major for the head, and then solo the choruses move from C, to Db, D, Eb, E, and F, etc. Whatever key is present for the last chorus can also be the key used to play the out head. You could also go all the way around the chromatic scale or circle of fifths and play the head in the original key.

This is a useful way to study jazz harmony and it helps you internalize and memorize tunes. Understanding the compositions as connected by intervals (for example: a major chord followed by a dominant chord up a M3, to a minor seventh chord down a P5) is useful, but so is roman numeral analysis of I to V7 of vi to vi. This helps the player understand, and play, the I chord (tonic) going to its relative minor (vi) but preceded by its V chord (a secondary dominant). This becomes really simple to transpose if understood this way.

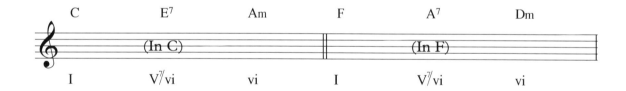

In C, this progression is C to E7 to Am; in F, this progression is F to A7 to Dm. For chordal instruments, this skill helps develop the ability to accompany singers in other keys. FOR ALL INSTRUMENTS

#23
HALF-NOTES ON CHORD TONES & TENSIONS:

As a great exercise to deepen your control over jazz harmony, in 4/4 time you should play half-note solos through entire real book tunes on the root. [That's an approach similar to Practice Idea #19.] There the focus was on the rhythm, where here it's about knowing and hearing the sound of the different chord tones and tensions over the harmony.

If the chord lasts for four-beats (an entire measure of 4/4), simply repeat the note. Then on the next chorus play the third of each chord. In the following choruses move on to the fifth, then the seventh, the ninth, eleventh, and finally the thirteenth.

After you've played through the tune for seven choruses (R-3-5-7-9-11-13), you've played all of the available notes in the diatonic scale, but in a different way. The half notes are great for grounding your playing into each measure and chord change, and the chord-tones and tensions exercise is great theory application and ear training.

Now you can choose one of those pitches (R-3-5-7-9-11-13) as a landing note for each harmony, but then you're free to improvise around it. For example, as you move through a tune in the real book, perhaps each measures line begins on the seventh of the underlying chord, and a connecting line can even end on the seventh of the following measure. FOR ALL INSTRUMENTS

#24
HARMONIC VAMPS:

Beginners often imagine that to play a challenging jazz composition, it is required to solo over the written harmonic rhythm -- the pacing of the chords -- and the entire form, as written. But great progress can be made by making vamps from tunes based on sections of the harmony that need improvisation work.

And if connecting the harmony together for an improvised solo is too difficult at full tempo, there is another strategy available rather than just slowing down the tempo. Try elongating each chord change. Where your tempo stays consisting for a 4-bar segment with a single chord in each bar, try two bars of each chord change (or 4 or 8!).

This allows you to settle into each harmony fully, and spend more time hearing the sonority and preparing to connect to the next change. For example a passage of four bars: Ebmaj7 - C7 - Fm7 - D7b9, could be augmented to eight bars of Ebmaj7-Ebmaj7-C7-C7-Fm7-Fm7-D7b9-D7b9, but practiced at the same original tempo.

The important takeaway is that jazz musicians should feel free to take any chords from tunes and make vamps for practice, ear training, and more. Based on the previous example, you might find that a very fast version of simply connecting eight-bars of Fm7 followed by eight bars of D7b9 would be the best choice for part of your available practice time. FOR ALL INSTRUMENTS

#25
THREE, FOUR, FIVE, AND SIX-NOTE VOICINGS:

For all improvisers, it's useful to understand jazz voicings, either for comping, jazz arranging and composition, or just to better understand jazz theory and harmony. For full seventh, ninth, eleventh, or thirteenth chords, it's beneficial to start with building 3-note and 4-note voices. After practicing "frames" of R-3-7 and 3-7-9 voicings in all keys and chord types, it becomes productive to find voicings using many of the strategies in this book. For example, with the tetratonics, pentatonics, or hexatonics, it's possible to create 3-note voicings by just choosing any three notes by register, and by ear.

For example, a D7b9 chord would be played as a line D-Eb-F#-A in tetratonics. Although limited, any three of those pitches -- in any register as an "open" or "closed" position -- can build a useable voicing. A possible 5-note scale choice for this chord (D7b9) could be an altered form of Bm pentatonic: B-D-Eb-F#-A. Any three notes from this pentatonic would make an interesting voicing.

For example, a chord like B-Eb-A or Eb-F#-A would give us (13-b9-5 and b9-3-5 on the D7b9). Then as you play (piano or guitar) or write voicings through a jazz tune, you just pay careful attention to voice-leading, avoiding awkward intervals, and connecting pitches by logical steps and leaps when you can.

Let's take a fully realized example: With the progression Cm7-F7-Bbmaj7, the C minor seventh to F dominant seventh can be converted to a hexatonic (double triad) of Eb and F, or the pitches Eb-G-Bb and F-A-C. The Bbmaj7 could convert to a Dm pentatonic (D-F-G-A-C, giving us 3-5-13-7-9 on the Bbmajor).

Let's create three-note voicings for each chord: G-C-Bb for Cm7, F-Eb-G for F7, and F-D-C for Bbmaj7. Apply your best instincts for voice leading. Here's one solution:

Now repeat these exercises - played or written -- for 4-note, 5-note, 6-note voicings, and beyond. The next stage in voicings is to move them through four-way close, four-way close double lead (8vb and 8va), and the drop 2, 3, 2/4 voicings, but that's beyond the scope of this book. (FOR ALL INSTRUMENTS)

#26
PRIMARY & SECONDARY CHORD SCALES:

One way to expand your ears, deepen your understanding of jazz harmony, and try out a range of possibilities with your improvisation is to realize that all chord symbols have a primary chord scale that works and then a number of other secondary choices and possibilities.

For example, inside a common ii7-V7-I progression in F, the most common choice for the ii7 chord (Gm7) is G dorian mode, or G-A-Bb-C-D-E-F-G. This is because a ii-V-I progression maintains all three chord scales as diatonic (one flat=F major), or G dorian to C mixolydian to F ionian.

In your improvised solo for secondary chord scales (after the initial G dorian), it's possible to choose G aeolian (natural minor G-A-Bb-C-D-Eb-F-G), or G phrygian (G-Ab-Bb-C-D-Eb-F-G). It's also possible to "borrow" Gm7b5 from minor (often called "mode mixture") and use G locrian (G-Ab-Bb-C-Db-Eb-F-G) or G locrian #2 (G-A-Bb-C-Db-Eb-F-G). [See #27 for a discussion about dominant choices.]

Every scale has its primary sound world, and over time learning, experimenting, and improvising with these secondary possibilities will really expand your playing. FOR ALL INSTRUMENTS

#27
DOMINANT CHORD SUBSTITUTIONS:

Beginning students often want to understand how chord substitutions work. Why use something else when the composer wrote A7? But with a lot of listening, you'll hear that jazz musicians often play a different chord, or improvise a different chord-scale over changes during the development of their solo. Since the solo is storytelling, by the time an improviser has played several choruses, substitutions are a way to add drama, or a different level of tension or release.

Of course, the opportunity around cadences gives improvisers the most opportunities for chord substitutions. As you continue to explore jazz harmony, you realize that at these cadential moments, a number of interesting possibilities arise if you make changes inside the primary and secondary dominants.

You do this by changing the chord quality of the seventh chord, with its tensions, which also changes the underlying chord scale. For example, in the key of A major, the V7 chord is E7 (mixolydian mode: E, F#, G#, A, B, C#, D, E) when applied with natural tensions (9,11,13).

At the moment of cadence of V-I, this chord can be changed to E7#11 (lydian dominant), E7b9 (symmetrical diminished), E7#9 (altered scale), and much more. Each chord-scale substitution introduces new colors and tensions, and can lead the improviser in new directions while soloing. FOR ALL INSTRUMENTS

#28
CYCLE OF FIFTHS CHROMATICS:

New improvisers often wonder the best way to start to incorporate more chromaticism in their improvising without going entirely into another key. A way to develop this control is to simply transpose your musical ideas around the circle of fifths. If you take a melodic idea and transpose up or down by a P5 -- over any chord quality -- you will begin to see notes that are still part of the original diatonic scale and with more cycles, more notes that are outside of the sound of the scale. You can practice these relationships by improvising with the original melodic fragment or scale then moving to other forms (transposed by P5's), and then returning to the original key center by ear.

For example, improvising with the scale G-A-B-C-D-E-F-G (G mixolydian) over a G7 chord is considered a primary diatonic choice. If you move the scale up a P5 to D mixolydian (D-E-F#-G-A-B-C-D) you have most of the same tones but you have now introduced the F#, a leading tone or chromatic approach-tone to the root of the G7. If you use A7 mixolydian (A-B-C#-D-E-F#-G-A) over G7, then you are also playing the C# over the G7 (which is #11) and you still have the F#, essentially chromatic approach tones to our original tonic and dominant.

Be sure to try this with all chord-types and scales making note of the relationships, and also try it with specific riffs and improvised lines. It's great ear training and it's easy to unravel so it makes it relatively simple to get back into the written key. FOR ALL INSTRUMENTS

#29

HARMONIC CENTERS, ANTICIPATIONS, AND HIERARCHY:

Sometimes when you let go of the strict chord changes on the page of a real book tune, a certain freedom emerges. For beginning musicians to simplify their approach and at the some time, begin to develop that freedom of more advanced improvisers, they need to allow the composer's original chord changes to be less rigid. To develop this ability, we can try a few different approaches.

- Tonal Centers: One way to do this is to simply improvise solos on tunes loosely based around the chart's basic key signature. For example, a tune in F major that cycles through several chords (including even secondary dominants!), could still be approached essentially as F major, with the player making some chromatic alterations by ear whenever necessary. This was an older style of entirely ear-based playing that some newer musicians forget to try.

- Before The Form: Another strategy is to anticipate the harmony of a chord change before it arrives in musical time. This has the effect of the soloist moving ahead, which is then resolved in the form when the rhythm section arrives at the chord change. Many players don't start working on anticipating chord changes very early in their development because they're focused on dealing with the chord of the moment, and not yet looking, thinking, or hearing ahead. These anticipations can give your playing a real sense of direction and momentum.

- Harmonic Hierarchy: A final, more intermediate-advanced concept of soloing -- which is a relatively common technique of modern players -- is to create some kind of harmonic hierarchy among the chords on a jazz chart. You can decide this ahead of time, or make the decision in the moment, but essentially you choose which chords are actually the most important harmonies in the piece. In a sense, you are deciding which harmonies you will play on, over, and towards, and essentially ignoring the others.

For example, if a tune has an "A" section with a number of chord changes that move from Dm to Gm to F to Dmaj7, you might decide -- almost arbitrarily -- that certain measures and harmonies are more important in this passage. For example, applying that practice idea to the passage below means that the improviser might connect a solo together on this section based entirely on the move from G minor to D major.

Experiment with this strategy and you will start to recognize it more and more in your favorite recordings. FOR ALL INSTRUMENTS

Now let's discuss a few ideas related to ear training.

10

Ear Training

"Imagination is more important than knowledge."
- Albert Einstein

#30
EAR TRAINING & SIGHT SINGING:

One of the best ways to use your real book for ear training is to sight-sing a tune by getting a single starting note, and then moving through the tune by intervals. This is a great way to internalize all of your ascending and descending intervals, and greatly improves your relative pitch. It also helps you hear ahead of your note choices when you're improvising lines.

With the real book, every page is a sight-singing exercise. For example, if your given starting note is an E4 followed by a C5 then to a B4 and an A4, then the ability to simply hear and sing a rising minor sixth followed by a descending minor second, and a descending major second is quite useful. You'll also begin to hear the relationships of these pitches to the underlying chords better as well. For example, if that entire line was written over an Am7 chord, then you'd be hearing the 5-3-9-R of the chord.

This can be a simple exercise, or depending on the chart of the lead sheet, a much more difficult one. You can also use your starting pitch to give you the root of the first chord change, and then simply sing the tonics of all the harmonies, by ear.

For a more advanced ear-training exercise, you could then sing the notes of the seventh-chord arpeggios on each of those changes. Remember all of this ear training and sight-singing work helps to deepen your connection with all of jazz harmony, and sharpens your ear toward chord tones, tensions, and the embedded intervals. It also helps speed up your reaction time for all of your improvisational instincts. FOR ALL INSTRUMENTS

SUGGESTED TUNES: Obviously this depends on your current ear training abilities, but try tunes like Blue in Green, Black Orpheus, and Summertime to start. For more advanced players, work your way through bebop heads like Billie's Bounce or When Will the Blues Leave, and take it from there.

#31
EAR-TRAINING WITH CHARTS:

Another great way to use your real book for ear training is to follow along with recordings and/or videos of your favorite players as they play standards and fake book charts. But the key to helping your ears, and also developing an ability to not get lost so easily, is to "hold" the form through the entire recording -- the intro, the head, the solos, the out head, and any vamps or coda.

If you additionally can snap your fingers on beats 2 and 4 (in 4/4 swing jazz tunes), or play along on your instrument, you'll also get the benefit of exploring your favorite players phrasing as you listen. It will help you hear where players play in the beat, how they phrase melodies, and by ear you will listen to the bass and chords to always know where you are in the form.

You can listen for motives, the relationship of improvised notes against the underlying harmony, and even places where the harmony has been stretched, anticipated, or like #29, given a new hierarchy. FOR ALL INSTRUMENTS

SUGGESTED TUNES: Try tunes with clear changes between the "A" section and the bridge because you'll always have an anchor during the soloing. Songs like Star Eyes, Watch What Happens, The Way You Look Tonight, and Chelsea Bridge, and others could work well here.

Next up, let's discuss transcribing...

11

Transcribing Solos

*"A man would do nothing if he waited until he could do
it so well that no one at all would find fault with what he has done."*
- Cardinal Newman

Like any artist, jazz musicians and vocalists can receive great benefits from making solo transcriptions of their favorite recording artists. There are a number of great lessons that come from transcribing jazz solos: issues of time feel, nuance, drama, note choice, phrasing, and much more.

Most jazz musicians understand the power of transcribing, and the overall impact it can have on their playing or singing, but realize that it's very time-consuming. If you already regularly transcribe, then you likely already see the changes in your playing or singing. If you don't regularly copy solos from recordings, here are a number of things to consider. Jazz musicians of all levels should consider making their own transcriptions of improvisations and improvised solos for a number of reasons. Whether you play saxophone, trumpet, guitar, upright bass, piano, or sing -- any jazz musician or vocalist can really benefit from the wide range of lessons learned when you make your own jazz solo transcriptions.

The Power of Transcriptions: What You'll Learn

- **Time Feel** - Sense of Swing 1/8's: Often the thing that draws you to transcribe a jazz solo in the first place is its sense of swing or overall time feel. The groove and subtlety of where the player places their eighth and quarter notes is a huge lesson for beginner and intermediate players. Think about the beat placement -- are they 'on top', 'right down the middle', or 'lobbing' slightly behind the beat, and do they change that placement as their solo progresses? This is such a signature part of an artist's sound, and this is what you want to study here. Think about the differences in the eighth notes of Miles Davis, Betty Carter, Dexter Gordon, Frank Sinatra, Joe Pass, Branford Marsalis, Joe Lovano, Mike Stern, Diana Krall, Michael Brecker, and others, and you can start imagine all there is to hear and learn.

- **Note Choice on the Chord Changes**: For many, the main reason to make a transcription of a solo is to understand the note choices of the recording artist. By looking at their melodic ideas in the context of the underlying harmony, you get a sense of their melodic and harmonic vocabulary -- and a peak into their sound world. Even though it was improvised by that person in the moment, it's a clear representation of how they hear the "changes" and deal with the underlying harmony. Generations of musicians have studied the Charlie Parker OmniBook (which is the well-known book of Parker's transcriptions) for this reason -- to see, on paper, what those lightning-fast note choices actually were.

- **Solo Phrasing:** This is powerful. Where does you favorite artist begin their improvised line? Do they start at different parts of the measure? How long are the phrases? How often do they go over the bar line - maybe even anticipating the next harmony? There are so many things to see here.

- **Sense of Drama -- Telling a Story with their Improvisations:** Great improvisers develop a solo over a series of choruses. It might sound logical, exciting, and more -- and often has a clear sense of drama and direction. Transcribing a solo can help you understand how this was accomplished. Did they leave a lot of space at first and then repeated ideas, only to develop into longer thoughts, with quicker subdivisions and more continuous lines later? Or maybe they started with fireworks and found an amazing way to settle down into a really provocative melodic development? Were there flashbacks to earlier ideas in their solo? Master improvisers also astound listeners with their ability to bring back an idea from much earlier in the solo, or even from the improviser they followed.

- **Nuance of an Improvised Solo:** As you learn to sing, play, and eventually fully notate your transcribed solo, you'll notice some really subtleties of nuance. Are there moments where notes are bent, scooped up, or dropped off? Are there places where a note has a growl, flutter, or a breathy quality? Think about Ornette Coleman or Billie Holiday here -- a Bb is not just a Bb if the color or timbre has been adjusted or inflected for a wide range of musical and emotional reasons.

Ear Training through Jazz Transcriptions

Ultimately a great reason to do any transcribing in the first place is the growth you'll experience in your overall ear training abilities. What material you learn to grab by ear from a CD, record, mp3, or other recording, will always help you respond quicker when you play live, do sessions, or make recordings of your own.

Even though a great deal of jazz transcription books are available, the greatest benefit of transcribing goes to the person who actually makes the transcription. Taking down the notes, figuring out the rhythms, and more is the necessary struggle that has the most results. Like any musician, jazz artists who have limited practice time and are always looking for good, solid, efficient jazz practice ideas understand the value of jazz transcriptions. I like to imagine that each project is essentially like taking a private lesson with the artist you are transcribing, whether they are still actually available for the lesson or not.

Up next, let's discuss some jazz composition ideas related to the real book.

12

Foundations of Jazz Composition

"What lies behind us and what lies before us
are tiny matters compared to what lies within us."
- Ralph Waldo Emerson

#32
SATB EXERCISES FROM FAKE BOOK TUNES:

A great composition and arranging writing exercise using your jazz fake book is to create simple four-part SATB chorale style arrangements, or exercises, of the tunes. Using the melody, as written, for the top voice, and use the chord-symbol to suggest the root, even though the moving notes of walking bass suggests inversions that would be totally fine.

For example, in an entire bar of A7, this exercise suggests you use A, C#, E, or G in the bass (inversions) or other notes in the chord scale (B, D, F#) as passing notes. Then the challenge would be, using great voice leading, to write the "alto" and "tenor" inner voices to help flesh out the harmony. If this is too simple, jazz composers can also expand from 4-part SATB writing, to SSATB, SSATTB, or SSAATBB, or any other useful combination.

What makes this a useful step is that you are essentially converting tunes from your real book into pseudo-Bach chorales. This skill is easily transitioned to original composition by simply writing an original top line (S), harmonizing it, and filling in the parts from there. FOR ALL INSTRUMENTS

#33
COMPOSED SOLOS:

Using the chord changes from any lead sheet, compose a full chorus of a solo using any strategies that you want (choose some from this book!), but try to build an organic solo with real sense of flow, and organic development. It's also possible to just compose some lines that could be over a single chord change.

Here's an example of eight bars of material written over the chord symbol Cm7 using a triad pair (Eb/F) from the hexatonic practice idea (#7). The concept here is that you can use your musical mind to create something you may never have improvised spontaneously. With a few rests, or edits, my Cm7 line could be the beginning of a new composition. It's also shown below over a Bm7.

Think about the rhythmic choices, the melodic connections to the chord changes, and other considerations like register and range. Since you don't have to worry about creating this "solo" in real-time, use all of the resources you have, and sing every note of it as you write it down to create the solo you wish you could create on the spot.

(The writing parameters here were to start in the middle at B4, eventually go up an octave to B5, and then go back to the original, and then the lower octave at B3, all using one hexatonic collection. It's an exercise, but I hope you see the possibilities.)

Bm^7 (line composed from D and E triads)

After you're finished, learn to play your solo (or lines) up to speed on the underlying tune or chord vamp, and use it as a launching point for several choruses of an improvised solo. If this proves to be difficult at first, then limit your choices with some composed-solo parameters. For example, you might decide that you want to write lines in all eighth-notes or quarter-notes and rests, that only uses pentatonic scales, for example. FOR ALL INSTRUMENTS

#34
MODULAR COMPOSITION USING REAL BOOK TUNES:

A great way to use your real book to generate fresh new compositions, is to consider any four-bar or eight-bar harmonic segment of a tune as a module that you can use in your music. Take out these segments inspired from a few different tunes, and you'll quickly build a song form. Then just compose a new melody on top of the new structures and play your piece.

While the modular part is possibly quick, the bulk of the work comes with trying to build a coherent melody over perhaps very disconnected, often non-functional harmonic modules. [This is also where that common chord exercise comes in handy! See Jazz Practice Idea #12.]

Here's how to start this exercise quickly. Think of four separate tunes that you enjoy playing over. Got them? Now take a four-bar harmonic segment -- four bars of the chord-changes only -- of each tune, and write them onto a new sheet of manuscript paper, or enter them into your notation software. Now decide a time-feel for your new piece (ballad, medium swing, even-eighths, fast swing, etc), and then play the chord changes over and over again to hear the new progression. You can go to the piano or guitar, obviously, but don't hesitate to use software/apps, if you don't have access to a chordal instrument.) Once the changes are in your ear, begin humming or singing a new melody, and then write down what you come up with -- and eventually your new tune is finished! Of course, you might have to connect together things you sing with other material you compose at the piano, guitar, or your primary instrument.

Other tips with this strategy: If you find that your module is too evocative of the original tune, then modulate part of it, swap out a chord, or use just a smaller fragment. It's entirely possible to use shorter two or three bar segments to build these new modular songs. FOR ALL INSTRUMENTS

#35
CONTRAFACT JAZZ COMPOSITIONS:

There has always been a strategy in jazz composition to write an entirely new tune over chord changes from a standard or other jazz composition. Technically called a contrafact, this explains all the "rhythm changes" tunes, the large number of tunes based on Gershwin's "I Got Rhythm". This tactic also helped the quick adoption of bebop, because although the melodies of the songs were new, many were based on chord changes of standards that rhythm section players would already know.

These types of tunes can be strict, where every chord of the original tune is used as is, or loosely applied, where the original tune suggests a basic harmonic framework, but is changed at the composer's discretion. Originally, contrafacts were composed on the forms of common standards, broadway songs, and well-known jazz tunes, but the system of composition can be applied to any jazz composition, even the most modern and contemporary. FOR ALL INSTRUMENTS

SUGGESTED TUNES: Try this on any tune that you really enjoy playing, where you have already internalized the sound of the chord changes. It can be a song without a lot of chord changes at first so that you have time to really stretch out and write, or it could be a chance to write a melody that has to deal with navigating its way through dense changes. It's also quite interesting to change the character of the piece and write an appropriate melody. For example, you could take tunes like Charlie Parker's Blues for Alice, Coltrane's 26-2, or Pat Metheny's Question and Answer and keeping the changes, rewrite all three as new ballads. You could also take ballads like the standards What's New or In the Wee Small Hours in the Morning, and All the Way, and tunes like Billy Strayhorn's Chelsea Bridge or Wayne Shorter's Infant Eyes, and make them into new up-tempo tunes (swing feel or Afro-Cuban).

#36
RECOMBINING JAZZ HARMONIES AND STRUCTURES:

A great exercise for jazz composers to create new works is to think of all the compositions in the real book as collages. Imagine any thirty-two bar song form in your fake book as a collection of thirty-two (32) separate measures of music.

Now imagine that these separate measures are puzzle pieces that can be recombined in any order. If you collect all of the similar chords in a song together into one section, you can transform a work that has a series of chord-changes into a piece with a vamp or a modal section. For example, if the song that you are recombining or reordering has 32-bars with four separate bars of Am7 scattered throughout the piece, your new re-ordered, restructured composition can begin or end with a four-bar section of Am7.

The two ways to approach this are to keep the original melody over the changes and just make an interesting new arrangement. Of course, it's also possible to combine these changes in interesting ways, and then compose your new original melody over the new structure. (For some inspiration related to this, check out the version of Stella by Starlight/Misstery on the recording "Directions in Music" (with Brecker, Hancock, Hargrove). FOR ALL INSTRUMENTS

13

Closing Thoughts

"As soon as you trust yourself, you will know how to live."
- Goethe

Well, these 36+ jazz practice ideas should keep us all quite busy for a while! And definitely feel free to make up your own hybrid exercises by combining two or more of the many strategies on this list.

Remember to always listen, listen, listen.... Listen to all the great recordings you can get your hands on. Listen to what you're really playing (and try to control it and develop it), and really listen to all the musicians around you when you play, rehearse, gig, or record.

Finally, always question 'authority' figures in music, always stretch your mind, and tune your ears to your realm of possibilities. Decide for yourself what players are interesting, useful, and compelling. Read about the lives of musicians, and you will be more inspired to practice because you'll realize the universal struggle that music requires of us.

And for those who are overwhelmed already with their practice, remember to always take things one step at a time, reward yourself for staying on schedule, and try to be as serious as you can about your commitment without going overboard. Enjoy the process more and try not to be impatient with yourself. And let me just say that really incredible progress can be made in a short amount of time by musicians willing to focus their time, and energy, and to work on improving the overall efficiency of their practicing. I have always believed that musical progress is just as much about hard work as it is about talent!

I'll wrap up with one of my favorite quotes, especially as it relates to jazz:

"It takes a great man to be a good listener."
-- *Calvin Coolidge (1872-1933), Vermont lawyer and thirtieth US President*

So thank you again for reading this, and best of luck on your musical journey.

THE
END

(Yes, you have reached the double bar: FINE)

14

Jazz Listener's Guide

"It takes two to speak the truth - one to speak and another to hear."
- Henry David Thoreau

Here's a short list of great jazz musicians and improvisers to explore for those who might need more suggestions for their own jazz listening. It's my personal, very subjective (!), and abbreviated list of interesting instrumentalists and vocalists spanning a range of traditional and historical players, but also includes a number of modern talented improvisers as well as some living masters.

Why put this kind of list together?

If you feel you need to broaden your listening, these are the musicians I would mention if we were having a conversation on person. If you ever wonder who else you should check out on YouTube, iTunes, Pandora, Spotify, Google Play, Amazon mp3s, or just whatever music to buy online or at some cool record store, then here are a few of my top suggestions -- in no particular order. (And yes, I know I left a lot of really great players off my list!)

Piano: Herbie Hancock, Art Tatum, Oscar Peterson, Chick Corea, Thelonious Monk,

Duke Ellington, Danilo Perez, Brad Mehldau, Joey Calderazzo, Dave Kikoski, Vijay Iyer, Keith Jarrett, Robert Glasper, Bill Evans, Borah Bergman, Matthew Shipp, Michel Camilo, Billy Childs, Bud Powell, Count Basie, John Medeski, Jaki Byard, Aaron Parks, Kenny Kirkland, Gonzalo Rubalcaba, Kenny Drew, Esbjorn Svensson, Sam Yahel, Ethan Iverson, Craig Taborn, Bruce Barth, Mary Lou Williams, Gerald Clayton, Geri Allen, Dave McKenna, Harold Mabern, Cyrus Chestnut, Benny Green, David Berkman, Bill Charlap, Cecil Taylor, Bud Powell, Wynton Kelly, Diana Krall, Don Pullen, Red Garland, Tommy Flanagan, Kenny Barron, Helio Alves, McCoy Tyner, Marc Copland, Niels Lan Doky, Makoto Ozone, Orrin Evans, Vince Guaraldi, Kenny Werner, Don Golnick, Herbie Nichols, Emmet Cohen, Jason Moran, Nitai Herkovits

Saxophone: Charlie Parker, Sonny Rollins, Michael Brecker, John Coltrane, Ornette Coleman, Joe Henderson, Kenny Garrett, Branford Marsalis, George Garzone, Jerry Bergonzi, David S. Ware, Chris Potter, Dewey Redman, Mark Turner, Rudresh Mahanthappa, John Zorn, Bob Berg, Eric Dolphy, Ben Webster, Sonny Rollins, Stan Getz, Dexter Gordon, Wayne Shorter, Joshua Redman, Seamus Blake

Bass: Paul Chambers, Scott LaFaro, Jaco Pastorious, Charles Mingus, John Patitucci, Ray Brown, Christian McBride, Santi Debriano, Dave Holland, Larry Grenadier, Jay Anderson, Mark Helias, Gary Peacock, Eric Revis, Richard Bona, Charlie Haden, Ron Carter, Victor Wooten, Avishai Cohen, George Mraz, Esperanza Spaulding, Marcus Miller, Scott Colley

Drums: Billy Higgins, Max Roach, Brian Blade, Dafnis Prieto, Bobby Sanabria, Antonio Sanchez, John Hollenbeck, Jeff Tain Watts, Tony Williams, Art Blakey, Paul Motian, Jack Dejohnette, Jeff Ballard, Ari Hoenig, Eric Harland, Billy Hart, Terri Lynn Carrington, Roy Haynes, Brian Melvin, Justin Faulkner, Joey Baron, Steve Gadd, Bill Stewart, Gregory Hutchinson, Jimmy Cobb, Art Taylor, Karriem Riggins, Horacio "El Negro" Hernandez, Alex Riel, Philly Joe Jones, Bobby Previte, Vinnie Colaiuta, Milford Graves, Al Foster

Guitar: Wes Montgomery, John Scofield, Lionel Loueke, Kurt Rosenwinkel, Julian Lage, Joe Morris, Mike Stern, Pat Martino, Bill Frisell, Jim Hall, Joe Pass, Charlie Christian, Pat Metheny, Django Reinhardt, Russell Malone, Peter Bernstein, Ben Monder, Paul Bollenback, Ulf Wakenius, Mick Goodrick, Charlie Hunter, Joe Pass,

Adam Rogers, Elliott Sharp, Derek Bailey

Trumpet: Miles Davis, Dizzy Gillespie, Lee Morgan, Art Farmer, Roy Hargrove, Wynton Marsalis, Nicholas Payton, Louis Armstrong, Kenny Wheeler, Donald Byrd, Wallace Roney, Clark Terry, Freddie Hubbard, Dave Douglas, Ryan Kisor, Brian Lynch, Ingrid Jensen, Tomasz Stanko, Cuong Vu, Wadada Leo Smith, Claudio Roditi, Arturo Sandoval, Tom Harrell, Don Cherry, Clifford Brown, Terence Blanchard

Trombone: Wycliffe Gordon, Conrad Herwig, J.J. Johnson, Kai Winding

Vocals: Dianne Reeves, Diana Krall, Kurt Elling, Esperanza Spaulding, Sarah Vaughan, Billie Holiday, Ella Fitzgerald, Cassandra Wilson, Gregory Porter, Gretchen Parlato, Tony Bennett, Cecile McLorin Salvant, Theo Bleckmann

***Of course, please check out the great music of all my friends and colleagues on the acknowledgment page as well!*

Here's how I like to approach listening and studying the music of these jazz artists: I start by finding a couple recordings of each artist to see if their playing or singing really speaks to me. If so, then I dive in fully! I think you get more out of listening by staying with one artist for a while, and checking out many things they have recorded to hear their approach in different bands, over different tunes, and in live performances versus studio albums. I also like to try to figure out the rough chronological order of their recordings, and if possible, listen in order from earliest to the most recent. That helps me have a hear a some aspects of their development as artists and improvisers, and can help me recognize some ways that their playing changes and evolves. And although it's fine to have your favorites, but make sure to listen to instruments/voices besides your own to broaden your influences and your overall familiarity with the music.

BEST OF LUCK WITH YOUR MUSIC!

Bonus Charts

So obviously I can't really include any real book tunes or standards in this book because of copyright restrictions, but I wanted to include a couple of my own jazz compositions as a bonus. Of course, I'm happy to have you play them, record them if you'd like, or use them in your studies. Here's some new-to-you music to apply some of the improvisation strategies, especially if you don't have a fake book with you. For reference, these are both 'C' concert charts.

- TWICE, by Andy McWain, Fuller Street Music (ASCAP)

- GOING TO STAY?, by Andy McWain, Fuller Street Music (ASCAP)

Twice

Andy McWain

Going To Stay?

Med. Swing

Andy McWain

Your Opinion

"Know thyself." - Linnaeus

Share Your Opinion with Others

If you found this book useful, informative, inspiring, or helpful in any way, please consider leaving NOT ONLY an online review where you bought it, but feel free to tell your friends, fellow musicians, music students, and others about it! Share the Amazon link to this book on Facebook, Twitter, Google+, and elsewhere. THANK YOU!

And please feel free to visit our website jazzpracticeideas.com. If you have any questions, comments, or thoughts that you'd like to share, you can contact me by email at this address: jazzpracticeideas@gmail.com, and also at (617) 528-9715. If you don't reach me, leave a voicemail, and I'll get back to you. [Yes, I just put a telephone number in this book!]

By the way, you really should also join our new Jazz Practice Ideas Facebook group at: http://www.facebook.com/groups/jazzpracticeideas to share what you're working on, and to read posts by a number of other musicians.

JAZZ PRACTICE IDEAS
with Your REAL BOOK

Acknowledgments

Special thanks to music copyist Brandon Carrita for his great work and attention to detail with the preparation (in Sibelius) of the music examples! There are also a number of people -- including many musicians -- whom I wish to thank for reading this book (or sections of it!) before it was released. Some made content and copy edit suggestions, and others were essentially pre-release beta readers who discussed the content, and approach of the book. I appreciate their input, suggestions, thoughts, experience, perspective, and more which has definitely made the final version much better. Any remaining errors, omissions, or general 'pockets of weirdness' are entirely my own fault!

Many thanks to:
Mike Caglianone
Brandon Carrita
Miles Flisher
Dino Govoni
Michael Hicks
Sofia Rei Koutsovitis
Michael Lavoie
Lance Van Lenten
Abby McWain
Marcus Monteiro
Hilary Noble
Mark Rasmussen
Jim Robitaille
Kareem Roustom
Riley Stockwell
Gordon Walters

Gratitude

A musician rarely has a chance to thank everyone (they can think of!) for lessons learned on gigs, concerts, and recording sessions. There are so many wonderful musicians I made music with and learned something tangible or intangible from, and for that I am quite grateful. Some of these people, I have played (or recorded with) for years, some for months, or in some cases just a single concert, recording session, or single gig -- although still memorable and fruitful for me in my own development. This is my attempt to thank the MANY musicians whose own playing and musical collaborations have helped to shape my playing, and my musical conception. You know who you are! Thank you.

About the Author

Andy McWain is a jazz pianist, composer, and writer from New England. He has performed improvised music throughout the United States, and in Germany, Switzerland, Japan, and China. McWain has taught jazz theory/improvisation, jazz history courses, jazz ensembles, and applied jazz piano at the University of Massachusetts Dartmouth for several years. McWain studied music at UMass-Dartmouth (B.M.), the Aspen Music School, and earned his M.M. in composition from the New England Conservatory of Music in Boston. His principal teachers included Lee Hyla, Michael Gandolfi, and Zhou Long for composition, and Anders Boström, John Harrison III, and Charlie Banacos for jazz improvisation. McWain received honors and fellowships for his music from the American Music Center, the American Composers Forum, the Atlantic Center for the Arts, ASCAP, the Massachusetts Cultural Council, the Akiyoshidai International Art Village, and Yaddo. His ensemble recordings as a leader and co-leader [Starfish, Vigil, Resemblance, Interpreter, Mishawum, and Live from Audible Think] on the indie label Fuller Street Music (fullerstreetmusic.com) and from Distrokid, feature mostly free jazz, avant-garde, collective improvisations, and original music. McWain launched jazzpracticeideas.com in 2011, and started the FB group: facebook.com/groups/jazzpracticeideas in 2014. Find out more at www.theandymcwain.com

"My playing, performing, recording, and teaching has taken me throughout the US, across Europe, and into Asia. With my writing, I'm happy to share what I've learned along the way with you." More information, other books on music, and an extensive list of jazz improvisation resources can be found at the site: jazzpracticeideas.com.

Other books by Andy McWain:

• Make Money Online with Your Music: Leveraging Web 3.0, YouTube, Google, Amazon, Facebook, Apple, Pinterest, Udemy, and other sites

• The Best Music Resources Online (You Should Know!): Web Resources for Musicians - Music Sales, Distribution, Teaching, Marketing, Production, and more (Creative Entrepreneurship Series)

Author's Note

"When you go in search of honey, you must expect to be stung by bees." - Joseph Joubert

I very often watch the Self-Publishing Podcast on YouTube which features full-time, indie-published authors Sean Platt, Johnny B. Truant, and David Wright talking about their approach to writing, strategy, and more. Among the many things I've learned from those wonderfully-irreverent and inspiring guys is the idea of including a brief Author's Note at the end of your books to give readers more personal insight into the process of writing this book. If you don't read this stuff, that's really OKAY. But if you're curious, here are your 'DVD extras' for this project.

As I mentioned on a 'Development Diary' blogpost on my writer site ajmcwain.com, the hardest part of this book was the daunting task of writing a jazz book at all. (There are so many good ones already.) The next most difficult was revising and personalizing the content after the first draft, because I first considered publishing this book under a pen name to just share it but not worry about credit. The more I realized that it might be nearly impossible, likely impractical, and/or downright silly to do that, I felt the freedom of "ownership." Save the pen names for other topics, but I'm writing my jazz book... under my own name. It's a daunting task, but this is my material based on my teaching, so it would be silly to hide the approach under an pseudonym. Then I knew I shouldn't try to just share this information in a direct, but perhaps even dry, way, but I could be more personal and real if it was actually me. I'm writing the opening of this note while I'm still rewriting the draft text in this way. This is ultimately led me to include the various quotes in the book that have inspired me for years.

But let's go back to that first hurdle... The real tricky thing about writing a jazz book, is of course that there are so many AMAZING jazz books already out there, and I have many of them. Sure, I believe that I have a unique angle here, but it's still a (mildy) daunting task. I choose to share my jazz practice ideas here for beginners and intermediate players largely because that's who I have been teaching all this time, but I greatly admire anyone who can easily create materials to help an advanced students or an accomplished player.

My hope is that any advanced or accomplished players who has stumbled upon this text still finds something fresh and/or useful. If that doesn't happen, maybe they'll encounter at least a new perspective that helps them in some way -- even if it's just in the way they assist new or intermediate players. [And no, I really do not claim to be an expert in jazz education, or in music education in general. I just wrote this particular jazz book. :)]

Notated musical examples are also the tough part of any music text. How many are needed? Are they all actually needed? What kinds of things do beginners need to actually see in notation? I don't know the answer to these questions and I imagine that the final text will just be my best guess for the length of this book. I DO know that if I add a lot of music examples, I could really change the length of the whole book, but I didn't want to just go for length. (Brandon did a great job with the examples I decided to include...)

What did arise from discussions with various beta readers was that perhaps more specific examples would be useful. That's when I made the decision to finally add tune suggestions to each of the thirty-six practice ideas. Since there are many versions of the real book from several publishers, and in multiple editions, I tried to suggest tunes across a very wide spectrum.

Of course, they're only for reference for those readers who appreciate some musical starting point with each topic. But, you'll also find that nearly any strategy can be used over any tune, so my suggestions were targeted simply for new practice sessions. For example, couldn't blues scales, pentatonics, hexatonics, tetratonics, and limited range soloing all be applied over Gershwin's Summertime? Yep. And with each strategy, you're expanding your musical mind, your technique, and your ears.

I also realized that once I finished this book, if I can use it in this format in my teaching, that will be the best test (for me) of its usefulness. I also like that fact that with the wide distribution platforms for ebooks, this could also be in the hands of beginning players all around the globe. That's pretty cool. A special thank you to the five anonymous American musicians and one anonymous French musician who pre-ordered this book before it was published. Those six orders provided some very useful motivation whenever I thinking about going to bed. See you over at jazzpracticeideas.com, or in our FB group, and of course, all best with your music.

Note: The paperback edition of this book has recently undergone some adjustments as well. If you're reading this, you'll notice that all of the blank left pages in the book -- necessary for chapter headings to start on the right side have been replaced by additional manuscript paper, making this practicing book hopefully even more useful for those working through it.

Thanks for reading. -- AJM

JAZZ PRACTICE IDEAS
with Your REAL BOOK

AS A **BONUS** FOR THE READERS OF THIS BOOK

I'd like to offer you a discount on any of these $10 blank music notebooks
from **Incredibly Useful Notebooks**:

Use this code: **MWB8593N** at any of these links
for $2 off any of these blank books...

Musician's Practice Journals:
https://www.createspace.com/5348457
https://www.createspace.com/5483557

Music Theory Notebooks:
https://www.createspace.com/5306095
https://www.createspace.com/5487195

Made in the USA
Middletown, DE
28 June 2021

43261273R00062